# The ABC's of Ability

## *an ABC book about the lives of adults with disabilities*

*created by Susan Powell*    *photographs by Larry Wells*

in collaboration with

**Cheryl Fryfield    Siobhan Harris    Sky Hendsbee
Tricia Lins    Peter Russell
Christina Tomingas**

**Foreword by Annabel Lyon**

Copyright 2012 Spectrum Press
ISBN 978-1-300-12636-2
Vancouver, B.C., Canada

**Spectrum** Press
A DIVISION OF SPECTRUM SOCIETY

# Dedication

*To all the individuals with disabilities and their families who have been our teachers*

## The ABC's of Ability: Foreword

The book you're holding in your hands is more than just an alphabet book. Certainly, it uses the alphabet to tell stories of daily life with humor and compassion. My big brother lives with a disability, and so much of this book was familiar to me. I especially loved G for Getting Around: "We know the bus schedule inside and out - just ask us!" That's my brother. And Y for Yakking - I love yakking about hockey and movies with my big bro.

Family, Belonging, Learning, Volunteering, Working, Exercising - these pages show the real lives of adults who can so often seem invisible in our communities.

But more than just an educational tool, this book is a celebration of the lives of adults with disabilities. With joyful pictures and heartfelt words, the reader is welcomed into the world of adults who are people first. "Our disability is only a small part of who we are."

Who should read this book?  I'd recommend it to anyone who wants to learn more about the life of someone in their community or family living with a disability.  I look forward to sharing it with my children, as a tool to teach them about their uncle's life.

But adults too will gain insight from this book.  Look around your community.  See the woman on the bus beside you, the man working in the restaurant, the friends going to the movies.  Once you've read this book, you'll never again think "disability."  You'll think "person, just like me."

Annabel Lyon

# Introduction

We are a group of six adults living with disabilities. Together we wrote this picture book. We want you to know about our lives. We have used each letter of the alphabet, along with a photograph, to describe what we think is important about being included in everyday life.

Three of us will appear in some of the photographs.

 Cheryl, who likes comedy movies.  She hopes to make more money one day so she can travel and buy special things, like shoes!

 Peter, who likes to watch good hockey on TV. He enjoys public speaking.  He wants people with disabilities to enjoy good quality lives.

 Siobhan (pronounced Shih-VON), who likes to read a lot. She loves the atmosphere of New York City.  She found working on this book a real challenge and at the same time enjoyed doing it.

To know about the rest of us go to the end of the book and read the authors' bios. We hope you like our book.

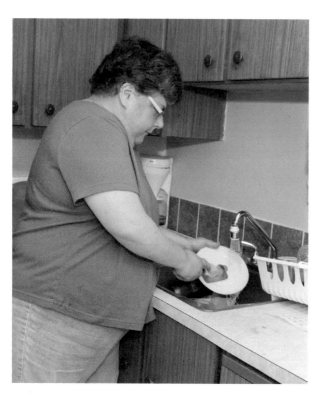

# Aa is for Ability

We have the **ability** to look after our own home, to learn a job, to manage our money and to make decisions.

# Bb is for belonging

**Belonging** makes us feel accepted and part of the community.  Being left out makes us feel lonely.

## Cc is for contribute

We think it is important to give back to our communities. We **contribute** in many ways, like mowing our neighbour's lawn.

## Dd is for dream

Just like you, we **dream** of winning the lottery, living in our dream home, traveling and having a family.

## Ee is for equal

To be **equal** means to be treated fairly. We want no more, no less.

# Ff is for family and friends

**Family and friends** are an important part of our lives. "I am a brother, an uncle and a great uncle!"

## Gg is for getting around

Our lives are very busy and full; so we must understand how to **get around.**

We know the bus schedule inside and out – just ask us!

## Hh is for history

In the past people with disabilities have been excluded from every day activities in the community. This **history** has left us with many hurt feelings. Today we are working with others to change this.

# Ii is for inspire

We **inspire** people to get out
and get involved.

It's one way we use our talents
to make the community
a better place for everyone.

# Jj is for job

We do real work for real pay. Having a **job** means feeling good about ourselves, and contributing.

# Kk is for key

Being independent is important to us.

"Having a **key** to my own place means I can come and go as I like."

# Ll is for learning

We are capable of **learning** many things. "Once I have learned something new I like to teach it to others."

# Mm is for motivational speaker

We present as **motivational speakers** at conferences and to high school students. "The students ask me lots of interesting questions."

# Nn is for neighbourhood

We are always out and about in our **neighbourhood**.

We use places like the bank, community centre, shopping mall, coffee shop and grocery store.

# Oo is for opportunity

**Opportunities** make life interesting and help a person grow.

We want a chance to learn new skills, meet new people and go to new places.

I am ...
• a hockey fan
• a good listener
• a reliable worker
• very atheletic
• someone who likes to sleep in
• humorous
• good at 10 pin bowling
• a country music fan
• a dancer
• a public speaker
• on many committees
• a man of many talents!

I am ...
• friendly
• caring
• a hard worker
• compassionate
• good at my job as a receptionist
• helpful
• a pro at making hamburger mush
• independent
• humorous
• knowledgeable about transit
• a Trekkie
• a huge fan of comed

am...
•a reader
•a walker
•an animal LOVER
dogs mostly
•a chatterbox
•a good sales
rep for art and
pottery
•a big fan of
LAW AND
ORDER
•someone who
likes to sleep
in
•a lover of New
York City
•someone who
remembers people
names
•a internet
user

# Pp is for being people first

We have hobbies, interests and feelings.

Our disability is only a small part of who we are. We are **people first**.

# Qq is for questions

We have lots of **questions** for people: How come people say we can't apply for a job? What makes people think it is okay to call us names?  Why do people think we can't learn?

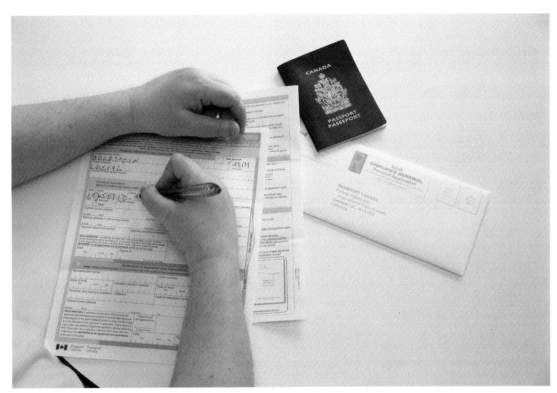

# Rr is for rights

We are citizens with the same **rights** as everyone else. We can vote, control our own money, be served in a restaurant and pick our friends.

## Ss is for self-advocate

As **self advocates**, we work hard to improve the quality of our lives.
If you want to know what we think about an issue, talk to us.

# Tt is for technology

We use it! Big-time! **Technology** is a huge part of our world. It keeps us connected to all our friends and events.

**Uu is for useful**

**Useful** means being helpful and doing things that benefit others. What letters in the alphabet have shown you how we are **useful** to our friends, families or community?

## Vv is for volunteer

We **volunteer** lots of our time to help out in the community. We contribute by caring for cats and dogs at animal shelters, working on committees, raising money and a thousand other things!

# Ww is for welcome

We believe the community is a place for everyone. Giving a warm **welcome** to someone is a way to make them feel glad about coming.

# Xx is for eXercise

We **eXercise** to stay fit and healthy. Sometimes we train to compete in swimming, bowling or softball tournaments.

**Yy is for yakking**

**Yakkety, yak, yak, yak**. We have lots to say everyday! We enjoy sharing fun times and having a laugh with our friends.

# Zz is for zest

Pow! Wam! We had a good time creating this alphabet book. We hope it lets you see and hear all the **zest** we have for life.

# Created by

**Cheryl Fryfield** has had many jobs. She has worked as baby-sitter, a camp counselor one summer, as a dishwasher and Quality of Life interviewer. She is now a receptionist. She likes to go to the gym, watch movies and read magazines. She wants to make enough money so she can travel one day.

**Siobhan Harris** has been a long time volunteer with seniors and was a representative for Pottery Works. She enjoys reading, music, computer games and hanging out with her friends.

**Sky Hendsbee** keeps busy through sports like baseball and swimming. He contributes many hours by being a board member and a DJ at dances. One day he hopes to have a family and live in his own apartment.

**Tricia Lins** puts in many hours on self-advocacy projects and initiatives.

**Susan Powell (facilitator)** is currently an independent consultant in human services and inclusive education. Her doctoral work was in transformative adult learning. She is an avid reader and likes to integrate children's literature into her workshops and classes.

**Peter Russell** wants to visit England one day (the birth place of his parents). He is an avid hockey fan, and likes to play sports, like softball, soccer, floor hockey and 10-pin bowling. He actively helps the community better understand people with disabilities.

**Christina Tomingas** enjoys hanging out with her friends and planning parties. She participates in track and field, gymnastics, 10-pin bowling and bocce. She currently works as a receptionist. One day she would like to be a teacher's assistant.

**Larry Wells (photographer)** is a retired educator who has been an avid photographer all his adult life. His photography can be viewed in stock photos for Maxx Images and in fine art prints for galleries and craft fairs. He now lives in Vancouver, B.C.

The ABC's of Ability team (Left to Right)
Sky, Christina, Siobhan, Susan, Peter, Cheryl, Larry and Tricia

## *Our process*

The United Nations now has a declaration outlining the rights of people with disabilities. One of these statements is about the right to participate in community.

Participation includes people with disabilities having a *heard* voice and discussing issues that are of importance to them. This picture book illustrates those sentiments and goes even further. Self-advocates not only informed the development process, but their voice is reflected in the words, images and sentences that compose the book.

The self-advocates began their work, for which they were paid, by exploring what is an ABC book and expanded the purpose of the book (as outlined by the facilitator).

Their purpose of the book is:

- To teach about the ways adults with developmental disabilities give to community by
    - Showing the many valued ways we contribute
    - Showing positive images
    - Dis-spelling myths
    - Inspiring others, including self-advocates

The group met for twice a month for several months. Many different processes were used to generate possible ideas and words for the book, i.e.: participants maintained a log about their involvement in community, filled out a capacity inventory, told a

 story about being excluded, responded to ABC books and responded to questions, particularly those used in A Focused Conversation Format.
Once an expansive word list was established A

Focused Conversation strategy was used to narrow the list. The group began to work on the ideas for each word at the time 26-29 words were agreed upon. Then the self-advocates were asked to respond to the question: What messages do you want the readers, the students, to take away with them after they have read that word? Self-advocates were also asked to suggest ideas for possible images.

Three of the self-advocates were employed to be models for the photo shoots. Every attempt was used to integrate people, places and activities that were an existing part of the lives of the self-advocates.

Self-advocates were asked to vote on book titles. When a final draft was developed a meeting was held with the self-advocates to determine if the book reflected images and statements that were faithful to their ideas.

The project set out to create a children's book that illustrated contemporary life of many adults with developmental disabilities. Their process also demonstrated the competency of adults with developmental disabilities, and their ability to engage in critical thinking tasks. But most importantly the self-advocates tell us how they see themselves, their wishes for themselves, and their valuable contribution to community.

# Keep Learning and Reading
### an invitation to discuss, write, read
### and check out additional resources

## Reading and Writing Activities

- ❖ **Anticipation Guide** is a comprehension strategy that is used <u>before</u> reading to activate students' prior knowledge and build curiosity about a topic. Give 4-6 key statements about concepts in the text and ask students to agree or disagree. Revisit each of the statements at the closure of the reading. Examples might be:
    - o People with disabilities can teach others about important things in life.
    - o People with disabilities need others to take care of them.
    - o People with disabilities use technology in their everyday lives.
    - o People with disabilities contribute to their community.
    - o People with disabilities need others to speak up for them.
    - o People with disabilities are like other people.

- ❖ **Focused Conversation** is a four-stage process to engage everyone in a conversation. There are 4 types of questions that are asked. Everyone in the group is asked to respond to the first question. Sample questions could include:
    - o What words or images stood out for you? (objective question)
    - o What surprised, intrigued or made you think? (reflective question)
    - o What does this book show about adults with disabilities? How does the title fit with the information in the book? (interpretive question)
    - o What can we do to collaborate with people with disabilities so they can have good lives in their community? (decisional question)

- ❖ **One Minute Write:** Ask students to write for one minute on the statement: What was the most important think you learned from the book?

❖ **Create your own ABC Book** on themes like diversity, community building, an historical event in your area. See what the students in Haida Gwaii created when they wrote "B is for Basketball"

**The Dolly Gray Children's Literature Award** was initiated in 2000 to recognize authors, illustrators, and publishers of high quality fictional and biographical children, intermediate, and young adult books that appropriately portray individuals with developmental disabilities. It offers an annotated list of books that present people with disabilities in positive and valued roles.

**Suggested Book Titles** about children and adults with disabilities:

- Crazy Lady by Jane Leslie Conly
- The London Eye Mystery by Siobhan Dowd
- Out of My Mind by Sharon Draper
- Mockingbird by Kathryn Erskine
- How Smudge Came by Nan Gregory
- Silent to the Bone by E.L. Konigsburg
- Rules by Cynthia Lord
- All-Season Edie and Encore Edie by Annabel Lyon
- Petey by Ben Mikaelsen
- Tru Confessions by Janet Tashjian
- Stuck In Neutral by Terry Trueman

## Sites to visit

- *www.notimeforflashcards.com*  - 30 books about being different
- *www.unicef.org/publications/index_43893.html* - It's About Ability: an explanation of the Convention on the Rights of Person with Disabilities
- *www.SpectrumPress.ca* - 101 Ways to Make Friends

**Acknowledgments – it's true, for a book to become real it takes the support, assistance and encouragement of lots of people. Many thanks to the people who gave generously to make our dream come true.**

Leigh Ariel, Barb Bradford, Jenny Chang, Marilyn Donaldson, Alecia Emery, Janine Hadfield, Dena Hickman, Jennifer Holley (at Foyer Maillard), Jule Hopkins, Chris Horrocks, Dana Horrocks, Nancy Hoyano, Joah Joseffson and Linian Joseffson, Penny Johnson, Sonia Kainth (at ConneXions), Tamara Kulusic, Doug McMillan, George Pearson, Shirley Pearson, Vicki Rothstein, Susan Russell, Keith Sims (at Forward Fitness), Kathy Soltani-Kohli (at Flight Centre), Spectrum Press, Ann Marie Walsh, Brian Wiebe, Linda Wiebe, Garfield Wilson (at Forward Fitness), Judy Wong, Doug Woollard

A DIVISION OF SPECTRUM SOCIETY

Spectrum Society is a not for profit organization successfully supporting adults with disabilities around greater Vancouver, British Columbia, for 25 years, in individualised, person-centred ways as they work, play and contribute in their homes, workplaces and neighbourhoods.

Spectrum Press is the social enterprise division of our organization, creating and distributing media by, for and about people with disabilities and those who care about them.   People with developmental disabilities contribute as paid researchers, writers and in other roles, such as models and book table hosts.  Our products support furthering interdependence and profits are currently focused on literacy and story-telling supports.

Spectrum Learning regularly presents work-shops on a variety of topics to staff, educators, families, self advocates and mixed community groups. We also provide facilitation, planning services and supported community based research. Each year we host best practice leaders to share information from around the world.

To learn more, visit these links!
www.spectrumsociety.org
www.spectrumpress.ca
www.101friends.ca
see us on Facebook or tweet
@101friendsBC
or call 604-323-1433